# THE
# PIPPITY- POPPITY
# POPCORN BOOK

## BY
## VICTOR E. CHEER

PRESBYOPIAN PRESS
Imprint of Rexdale Publishing Company
P.O. Box 563
Hackensack, New Jersey 07602-0563

www.PresbyopianPress.com

The Pippity-Poppity Popcorn Book
Second edition ©2003

Library of Congress Control Number: 2001095980

ISBN: 0-9724651-3-8

Printed in the United States of America

Published by:  Presbyopian Press
Imprint of Rexdale Publishing Company
P.O. Box 563
Hackensack, New Jersey 07602-0563

Edited by: Karen Rice

Cover and Book Design: Jonathan Gullery
Budget Book Design.com
New York, New York


www.PresbyopianPress.com

## Florence Edith Gillum
## 1895-1975

Grandma lived across Salt River, next door to the woods that grew at the end of a long dusty road. When our 1947 Plymouth drove out of the last winding gully, my brother and I would stop bickering in the back seat of the car and eagerly look for Grandma. There she would be, like magic, standing outside her real log cabin amid her yellow rose garden, smiling and waving to us.

There was nothing to do at Grandma's and everything to do at Grandma's. She had no neighborhood kids to play with, no television, no computer, and not even a telephone. Instead, we planted the garden, fed the chickens, slopped the hogs, watched out for poisonous snakes, and picked the corn, cherries and blackberries. We weren't good at hoeing the garden, though we tried, but we were powerfully good at eating her fried chicken dinner and blackberry cobbler.

Most of the time we didn't recognize the little life-long lessons in love, responsibility, patience, and loyalty that Grandma dispensed so easily. But these lessons from our Cherokee grandmother, who lived across Salt River, next door to the woods that grew at the end of a long dusty road, were the foundation of our knowing who we were in our big world. It was never a long trip to Grandma's house and oh how we wish we could visit her just one more time!

# Table of Contents

# Popcorn:
# The Gift That Was Better Than Gold

Popcorn is so much a part of our lives today that we sometimes forget it really is one of the greatest gifts the Native American cultures gave to the entire world. While corn had been grown in China, India and Sumatra many years before Christopher Columbus discovered the Americas, it was his discovery of the Native Americans and their use of corn that ultimately delighted the rest of the world. The Aztec, Incan, and Mayan Indians cultivated corn more than 5,600 years ago, along with beans and squash. However, corn was an extremely versatile and important food source for the natives, and one they learned thoroughly to enjoy. They chewed the sugar-filled corn plant leaves as their chewing gum. They ate the immature corn as a vegetable. And they ground the mature dried corn kernels into flour. It served their needs well, since it could be used fresh or dried. It could also be stored for later use, and it could be used to create a fermented beverage.

America's favorite snack food evolved from a wild grass known as *teosinte* many centuries ago. Upon meeting the natives, Columbus found they were familiar with approximately seven hundred different varieties of corn. The wild popcorn known then doesn't exist any longer. Our popcorn today comes from several hybrid varieties of corn that have been developed by scientists. These new hybrid varieties do not grow in the wild, and they require man's proper cultivating talents to produce a crop.

## A Little History

Archeologists have found evidence dating back to 1200 A.D. that corn was grown in North America near Ontario, Canada. One of the things that makes corn so valuable is its ability to grow in so many different climates.

Explorer Christopher Columbus discovered the Taino people, inhabitants of the islands in the Northern Antilles, in 1492. He learned the Taino people grew a grain crop from a native edible grass seed. The Taino called their grain crop *mahis*, which was translated to mean source of life. Over time their word *mahis* changed phonetically into the word we use today, maize. Later European explorers used the German word *korn* to describe the small fleshy nuggets on the corn cobs, and the Latin word *granum*, which was an all encompassing term for grains. Columbus also reported that the natives tried to sell popcorn to his ships' crew. And when it was time for Columbus to leave the Taino, they gave him corn to take on his return voyage to Spain. It was a gift of food that would travel easily without spoiling.

The Spanish Conquistador Hernan (Hernando) Cortés became acquainted with popcorn when he invaded Mexico in 1519. He found the Aztecs using popcorn not only as a food and a decoration for their native dress but also as jewelry. They were also using popcorn to ornament their statue of Tlaloc, their god of maize, rain and fertility.

The 16th Century Spanish missionary Bernardino de Sahagún was assigned to the College of Santa Cruz de Tlaltelolco by his church superiors around 1529. There he was directed to compile, in the Aztec language, everything relating to native history and custom. During his fifty years of missionary work to the natives, he reported seeing young Aztec women dancing with garlands of popcorn upon their heads at special ceremonies.

He also reported the Aztecs honored their gods who protected fishermen by scattering parched corn. This they called *momochiti*. When the corn was popped it burst open and resembled a white flower. The Aztecs felt this popped corn was actually hailstones given to the god of water.

Then in 1612, Frenchmen exploring the Great Lakes region of North America reported the Iroquois using popcorn. The Iroquois popped their corn in special pottery that was placed in heated sand. They also prepared a soup and fermented a beverage from popcorn.

It is generally said that Quadequima, brother of Chief Massacoit of the Wampanoag tribe, took a gift of popcorn to the first Thanksgiving Feast with the colonists in Plymouth, Massachusetts in 1621. However, according to the Plimoth Plantation - Museum of 17th Century Plymouth, this just wasn't the case. History was revised incorrectly when Jane G. Austen published a book entitled *Standish of Standish* (1889). She had written a breakfast scene in the book entitled "First Thanksgiving Day", which listed popcorn among the dishes at the feast. In reality, popcorn was not on the menu that day, but Ms. Austen's book became so popular that succeeding generations accepted this error as fact and perpetuated the myth. Only now is the truth becoming known.

In 1650 we have information from Spanish Jesuit missionary, Bernabé Cobo. He was called the ablest and most thorough student of nature and man in Spanish America during the 17th century. His important writing, "Historia General de las Indias", reveals detailed and reliable information about the natives and their culture. So when Cobo wrote of the Peruvian Indians, "They toast a certain kind of corn until it bursts. They call it *pisancalla* and use it as a confection." the academic world paid attention.

Corn's popularity received a great assist from Thomas Jefferson, the third President of the United States. Mr. Jefferson was also an agriculturist and an inventor. One of his inventions was a "moldboard plow of least resistance" in 1814. He had observed European plow designs in France, and after several years he succeeded in perfecting a design that used a lighter piece of machinery that could easily be drawn by animals. He said the plow was "so light that the two small horses or mules draw it with less labor than I have ever before seen necessary. It does beautiful work and is approved by everyone."

Mr. Jefferson's plow design would now give farmers the ability to clear and cultivate large areas of ground. Farmers would be able to realistically manage larger tracts of land and cultivate corn. Jefferson never sought to turn a profit on his machine and did not patent it. However, he sent many models of the new plow to his friends at home and abroad and thereby popularized the plow. His agricultural contribution for the moldboard plow was recognized in James Mease's Domestic Encyclopedia (Philadelphia, 1803).

While the natives and the colonists had been eating corn for a long time, it wasn't until 1846 that the first known cookbook to mention popcorn was published. By 1916, however, people were busily engaged in experimenting with corn and enjoying at least one new popular recipe known as the popcorn omelet. Likewise, the sale of seed for popcorn cultivation first appeared in farmers' seed catalogs about 1880. The average person would now have easy access to getting seed for cultivation.

Americans continued developing new popcorn recipes. Eventually one of the most popular confections of the latter part of the 19th century was born: the popcorn ball. These new popcorn balls were sold by street vendors, who flavored them with orange and lemon juice, sugar, roses, peppermint, honey and molasses. The only known limit on this exciting new confection was a person's imagination. There were many other popular recipes using popcorn: popcorn brittle, popcorn cake, popcorn pudding, popcorn fritters, and popcorn cereal. And then there was, of course, Cracker Jacks, the confection invented by Frederick William Rueckheim, a German immigrant. Cracker Jacks was a mixture of popcorn, molasses, and peanuts and it became famous by its mention in the 1908 song *Take Me Out To The Ball Game*.

During World War I and World War II, the Office of Price Administration (OPA) rationed commodities that were needed for the war effort and commodities that were often imported from other parts of the world. One item rationed was sugar. It was now necessary for families to use sugar substitutes such as honey, corn syrup and molasses for their table consumption and recipes because their bi-weekly sugar ration was only one pound.

Families who previously had used sugar to make confections now remembered the popcorn balls. Popcorn balls could be made with very little sugar or by using corn syrup and molasses. By stretching out the amount of sugar used it was possible to have a deliciously sweet treat while complying with the ration system.

Shortly after the close of World War II, archeologists working in Bat Cave, located in west central New Mexico, found ears of corn that were sized from smaller than a penny to about two inches across. Carbon dating of these ears of popcorn placed them at about 5,600 years old. Other scientists found an 80,000-year-old corn pollen fossil two hundred feet under Mexico City that is nearly identical to today's corn pollen.

Scientists in Peru found grains of popcorn, perhaps one thousand years old, while working in tombs on the East Coast. The amazing thing about their discovery was that these popcorn kernels were so well-preserved that they could still be popped!

Still another exciting discovery took place in southwestern Utah. There scientists found a thousand-year-old popped kernel of popcorn. It was found in a dry cave that had been inhabited by the predecessors of Pueblo Indians.

## 21st Century Corn

The discovery of corn dramatically changed civilization around the world. Ironically, Columbus was focused on discovering great wealth in the form of gold or spices, and did not seem to realize the vast importance of this wonderful grain that feeds not only people but also their animals.

Today, popcorn is an important American crop. American farmers grow over forty percent of the world's corn. There are twenty-five states growing this important grain crop. The top five corn-producing states are Iowa, Illinois, Nebraska, Minnesota, and Indiana. When we add Wisconsin, Michigan, Ohio, Kentucky, Kansas, and Missouri to the list, we have what is commonly known as the Corn Belt. If you are ever able to drive through this part of the country during growing season you will witness rows upon rows and fields upon fields of this marvelous plant being cultivated.

While most of the corn is grown in the Corn Belt, corn is an extremely versatile crop that can be grown on every continent in the world except Antarctica. It is successful as a grain crop because it can grow in areas with heavy annual rainfall or in areas with extremely light rainfall. Its versatility has made it the largest crop in America both in acreage planted and in the total value of the crop.

About seventy percent of all the corn purchased in America is purchased for home consumption. The other thirty percent purchased is eaten at the movies, county fairs, baseball games, and other group activities. The popular popcorn street vendors of the 1890's have moved into the local shopping malls and supermarkets, and have set up shop in parks. We love popcorn. On an average, Americans consume nearly seventy quarts of popcorn each year for every man, woman, and child living here.

Today we have special popcorn kettles and microwave popcorn available for our use. The natives had several methods for exploding their popcorn too. Some put the corn kernels directly onto hot sand, waited for it to pop, and then collected all the white popped corn.

The Papago Indians of Arizona used eight inch wide pottery pots known as *ollas* that were constructed so as to sit on the fire and allow the corn to pop. This style of popping corn was more sophisticated since the *ollas* had a vented lid that kept all the popcorn within the pot. Some natives added oil or fat to the corn before placing it in *olla*. These *ollas* date back approximately 1,500 years and were used by the South American Indians as well. The use of *ollas* is a clear link in popcorn's history, and they are probably the forerunner of our modern-day microwave popcorn.

One day in 1945, a self-educated inventor, Percy Spencer, was working in a Raytheon Manufacturing Company in Waltham, MA. Laboratory. He was testing a new vacuum tube dubbed the magnetron that was to be used in a newly developed radar system for the military. Spencer's curiosity was tweaked when a candy bar melted in his pocket during the test. He wanted to know what would happen to popcorn when exposed to high-frequency radio waves. He was in for a big surprise and a lot of freshly popped corn all over his lab. Popcorn had played an important role in the discovery and initial recognition of what would become our modern day microwave.

Just like us, some natives learned to be time efficient while popping corn. The Winnebago natives pulled the husk back, speared the corn cob while the dried popcorn was still intact, and then placed the ear of corn directly on the fire. The result was that the kernels popped while still on the cob, thereby saving them the trouble of gathering up the popcorn.

Still other natives cut the ear of corn from the corn stalk leaving a long "handle". Once the ear was dried the natural handle was used to place the ear into the fire for popping. After the corn had popped on the cob it was possible to use the "handle" and eat popcorn.

### The Giving Plant

Our long history with popcorn is the record of a love affair of enormous proportion. Popcorn was the gift, given directly from the native cultures of North and South America, that has been not only a food source that has sustained us and our livestock, but also a gift that keeps on giving.

Research scientists continue to find new ways of utilizing corn. They are developing fuels and biodegradable plastics from corn products. Discoveries in these areas will assist the world in effecting sound ecological programs and will positively affect the way we live in the future. One such important discovery is Ethanol. Ethanol is an environmentally friendly, renewable fuel source derived from corn. It can be used alone or in combination with gasoline and can greatly reduce our dependence on foreign oil. If we need more fuel, we can grow more corn. Researchers have also developed a tire made in part from corn products. These products continue to make the automobile environmentally friendly.

Other researchers have created products that provide cleaning solutions and hand soap for the home. These products are made in total or in part from corn. The next time you hold a plastic cup, a plastic dish or a golf tee, remember that there is a very good possibility these were made from corn. These biodegradable plastics are even used in disposable diapers.

The medical community is especially interested in a new product called AmaizingOil. It is a new corn oil that is produced by removing the fiber from the hull of a corn kernel and is thought to have cholesterol reducing properties.

Another exciting project scientists are working on is the development of a white corn fiber gum. This gum is not the bubblegum we chew. It is generally a tan or brown color and is used to thicken food products such as soups, salad dressings, and spreads. The researchers have developed a white corn fiber gum that is far more commercially attractive than the tan or brown color gum. Zea mays is the scientific name for corn and so researchers have named this product Zeagen

Corn can also provide an alternate heating system for our homes. Corn burning stoves are in production and available for purchase now. The corn burns clean and reduces air pollution. It also provides an inexpensive, controllable heating system. If we require more heating fuel, we will grow more corn.

The popcorn you share with your family is quietly holding many secrets. Its secrets are a history of native grasses and cultures, discoverers, conquistadors, farmers, archeologists, inventors, and researcher scientists. Popcorn, the special corn that can jump three feet in the air while popping, is an important strand in the fabric of man's history. And you, as a popcorn lover, join the thousands of people who have enjoyed popcorn throughout the centuries.

## Basic Bliss

### Ingredients

2 1/2 qts. Popcorn
1/4 lb. Butter
Salt as desired

### Directions

Set warm popcorn aside. Melt butter and drizzle over popcorn.
Toss lightly until all kernels are coated. Add salt to taste.

## Popcorn Soup

### Ingredients

1/4 lb. Butter
2 tbsp. Celery (minced)
2 tbsp. Onion (minced)
3 tbsp. Flour
5 cups of Milk (cream may be substituted)
1 can of Cream Style Corn
Seasoning as desired
Freshly popped and buttered popcorn for crouton garnish

### Directions

Sauté the onion and celery in butter until the onion is transparent.
Combine flour with one cup of milk (as if you were making gravy)
making sure there are no lumps. Add this to the celery and onions.
Gradually add the remaining milk, stirring constantly. Cook mix-
ture until it thickens and is smooth. Add the cream style corn.
Serve hot after adding popcorn garnish.

# Heavenly Hash Popcorn

## Ingredients

2 1/2 qts. Popcorn
1/2 cup Kahlua
1 cup Granulated Sugar
3 tbsp. Cider Vinegar
3 tbsp. Unsalted Butter
3/4 cup Cashews

## Directions

Set warm popcorn aside. Combine Kahlua, sugar and vinegar and bring to a boil. Stir until sugar is completely dissolved. Add the butter and bring to 300° (hard crack stage on a candy thermometer). Pour over warm popcorn and toss lightly until all kernels are coated. Add cashews and cool. Store in an airtight container. Do not refrigerate.

# Ketchup Korn

## Ingredients

2 1/2 qts. Popcorn
A bottle of your favorite ketchup (salsa may be substituted)
Salt as desired

## Directions

Set warm popcorn aside. Drizzle or squirt ketchup over popcorn. Toss lightly until all kernels are coated or leave ketchup concentrated in some areas. Add salt to taste.

## Company's Coming Popcorn

### Ingredients

1 bag of Microwave Popcorn (popped)
1 cup of Cheddar Cheese (shredded)
1/2 cup each Olives, Celery, and Radishes (sliced)
1/4 cup Green Onion tops (sliced)
8 slices of Bacon (crispy-fried and crumbled)
1 can Water Chestnuts (8 oz., sliced, well drained)
1 cup Mayonnaise

### Directions

Set warm popcorn aside and remove all "Old Maids". Combine ingredients at the last minute and toss.

*The unpopped kernels of popcorn in a pot are called "Old Maids" and "Spinsters".*

## Crispy-Crunchy Popcorn

### Ingredients

2 qts. Popcorn
1/8 cup Bacon Drippings (cooled)
1/4 cup Butter (melted)
6 slices Bacon (crispy-fried; chopped)

### Directions

Set warm popcorn aside. Mix butter, bacon drippings and bacon pieces; drizzle over popcorn. Toss.

# High Voltage Popcorn Snack

## Ingredients

2 1/2 qts. Popcorn
1 cup Chow Mein Noodles
1/2 cup of Peanuts (shelled and roasted)
1/3 cup Peanut Oil
2 tbsp. Soy Sauce
1/4 tsp. Cayenne Pepper
1/2 tsp. Garlic Powder
1/8 tsp. Sugar
1/2 tsp. Ground Ginger
1/2 tsp. Sesame Salt

## Directions

Combine popcorn, chow mein noodles, and peanuts. Mix remaining ingredients together; pour over popcorn. Toss. Toast in a preheated oven of 350° for 5 minutes. Stir gently as needed.

# Hotted-Up Corn

## Ingredients

2 1/2 qts. Popcorn
1/4 cup Butter (melted)
1/4 tsp. Cayenne Pepper
1/2 tsp. Garlic Powder
l tsp. Lemon Pepper
1/2 tsp. Onion Powder
1 tsp. Paprika

## Directions

Pour melted butter over popcorn.
Mix dry ingredients together; toss over the popcorn.
To make popcorn very crispy, place in a 300° oven for a short time.

## Zesty Popcorn

### Ingredients

2 qts. Popcorn
1/3 cup Butter (melted)
1/4 cup Dill (freshly chopped)

### Directions

Set warm popcorn aside. Add dill to butter and drizzle over popcorn. Toss.

*There are five types of corn. They are Dent, Flint, Sweet, Flour and Popcorn. Dent and Flint are commonly called "sweet corn" and used to feed animals. Sweet, Flour and Popcorn are used to feed humans. Only Popcorn truly "pops".*

## Flaming Crunchies

### Ingredients

2 1/2 qts. Popcorn
12 oz. Mixed Nuts (shelled)
1/4 cup Margarine or Butter
6 tsp. Vegetable Oil
2 tsp. Curry Powder
1 tsp. Salt

### Directions

Combine popcorn and mixed nuts; set aside. Melt butter, add curry powder and salt, being careful not to burn. Pour butter mixture over the popcorn; toss to cover corn.

# Pippity-Pop Popcorn

## Ingredients

2 qts. Popcorn
1/2 cup Butter (melted)
1 pkg. Dried Yeast

## Directions

Set warm popcorn aside. Pour butter and yeast over popcorn; toss.

# Peppered Corn

## Ingredients

3/4 cup Popping Corn (kernels)
2 tbsp. Corn Oil
2 tbsp. Olive Oil
2 Garlic Cloves (split)
2 tbsp. Butter
2 tsp. Black Pepper (coarsely ground)
Dash Cayenne Pepper
1 Garlic Clove (minced)
1/4 cup Hot Pepper Sauce

## Directions

Place corn and olive oils in a heavy cast iron Dutch oven if possible, or very heavy pot. Heat oils until a kernel of corn pops when added. Add split garlic cloves along with the popping corn. Cover the pot and gently shake. When the popcorn begins to pop, shake the pot with enthusiasm so the corn doesn't burn; continue until all the corn is popped. Remove from the stove. Mix the melted butter and hot pepper sauce together; pour over the popcorn. Toss the popcorn gently adding the minced black pepper, cayenne, minced garlic and salt.

*Early settlers ate popcorn for breakfast.*

## South of The Border Popcorn

### Ingredients

2 qts. Popcorn
1 cup Tortilla or Corn Chips (crumbled)
3 tsp. Butter
2 tsp. Taco Seasoning Mix
1/2 cup Cheddar Cheese (grated)

### Directions

Place popcorn and chips together in a bowl. Set aside. Melt butter; add taco seasoning mix. Pour butter and taco mixture over popcorn; toss and sprinkle with cheddar cheese.

*Popcorn has more protein than any other cereal grain.*

## Tea-Time Popcorn

### Ingredients

2 1/2 qts. Popcorn
1/4 cup Butter (melted)
2 tbsp. Iced Tea Mix (instant, lemon)
1 tbsp. Sugar

### Directions

Place popcorn in a bowl. Combine instant tea and sugar; mix with butter. Drizzle over popcorn and toss.

# Party-Hardy Popcorn

## Ingredients

1 1/2 qts. Popcorn
1/3 cup Butter (melted)
1 tsp. Worcestershire Sauce
1/4 tsp. Garlic Salt
1/4 tsp. Onion Salt
1 cup Pretzel Sticks (thin)
1/2 cup Peanuts (shelled, salted and roasted)

## Directions

Combine popcorn, pretzels and peanuts. Place in a bowl and set aside. Combine remaining ingredients and stir. Drizzle over popcorn mixture and toss to coat evenly. Place on a baking tray in 250° oven for 45 minutes; stir every 10 minutes.

*Popcorn kernels come in shades of gold, red, black, and off-white.*

# Nutty-Not-Stuffy Popcorn

## Ingredients

3 qts. Popcorn (unsalted)
1/2 cup Brown Sugar
1/2 cup Butter
1 cup Walnuts (chopped)

## Directions

Combine popcorn and walnuts; set aside. Combine brown sugar and butter; cream. Add sugar mixture to popcorn mixture until coated. Bake in 350° oven 10 minutes.

# El Paso Fevers

## Ingredients

4 qts. Popcorn
3 small Dried Red Chilies
6 3/4 oz. Roasted Peanuts (shelled)
3 1/4 oz. Roasting Pepitas (1 package)
6 tbsp. Butter
3/4 tsp. Garlic Salt

## Directions

Set warm popcorn aside. Place butter, chilies and peanuts in a skillet and cook over low flame for 5 minutes. Remove the chilies. Add the pepitas to butter mixture and pour over popcorn. Sprinkle with garlic salt.

# Dubya Trubya

## Ingredients

2 qts. Popcorn
1 pkg. Pretzels (the trouble)
2 tsp. Ground Chili Powder
2 tsp. Ground Cumin
2 tsp. Paprika
1 cup Monterey Jack Cheese (shredded)

## Directions

Set warm popcorn aside. Mix all other ingredients together and toss with the popcorn.

## Jimmy Hot Corn

### Ingredients

2 qts. Popcorn
1 tsp. Mustard Powder
1/2 tsp. Thyme (ground)
1/4 tsp. Black Pepper (ground)
Dash Cayenne Pepper
1/2 tsp. Salt

### Directions

Set warm popcorn aside. Combine all other ingredients and sprinkle over the popcorn. Gently toss kernels to distribute the spices.

## Out-Of-The-Frying-Pan

### Ingredients

1/3 cup Popping Corn (kernels)
1/3 cup Cooking Oil
4 Dried Chilies
1 Garlic Clove (quartered)
1 tsp. Cumin Seed
3 tbsp. Seasoned Hot Oil
1/3 cup Parmesan Cheese (grated)
1 tsp. Paprika
1/2 tsp. Salt

### Directions

Combine the cooking oil, chilies and garlic clove in a saucepan to
cook over a low flame for 3-5 minutes. Let cool for 10 minutes and
then strain the oil. Use 3 tbsp. of this seasoned hot oil to pop corn.
After the corn is popped you can combine all the other ingredients
together and mix with the popcorn. Toss the popcorn gently so that
all the kernels are covered evenly.

## Jungle Powder Keg

### Ingredients

5 qts. Popcorn
1 cup Banana Chips (dried)
1/2 cup Peanut Butter (chunky style)
2 tsp. Vegetable Oil
1 tsp. Soy Sauce
1/4 tsp. Cayenne Pepper
1/4 tsp. Garlic Powder
1/4 tsp. Ground Garlic

### Directions

Place popcorn and banana chips in an oven pan. Combine and blend peanut butter and vegetable oil in a saucepan. Add seasonings and heat. Pour mixture over popcorn and banana chips then place in 300° oven for approximately 10 minutes. Stir as needed so all kernels will absorb flavor.

## Hot & Bothered Popcorn

### Ingredients

1 cup Popping Corn (kernels)
1/3 cup Peanut Oil
1/2 cup Jalapeño Peppers (sliced)and Juice
Salt (if desired)

### Directions

Place oil in large pot and add Jalapeño peppers with juice. Pop the corn in the hot oil and Jalapeño mixture.

# Hot Under The Kernel Popcorn

## Ingredients

2 qts. Popcorn
1/4 cup Butter (melted)
1/4 cup Parmesan Cheese (grated)
1/2 tsp. Chili Powder
1/2 tsp. Garlic Salt
1/4 tsp. Onion Powder
1/2 tsp. Paprika

## Directions

Set warm popcorn aside. Place all other ingredients together and mix; toss with popcorn. Put popcorn mixture onto a cooking tray and bake at 325° for 7-10 minutes. Stir if needed.

*Each popcorn kernel ideally should have between 13 and 14.5% moisture within to pop well. When the kernel is heated to 400° this moisture turns into steam and explodes the kernel. The soft starch inside the kernel turns inside-out and becomes approximately 40 times its original size.*

# Onion Patch Popcorn

## Ingredients

2 qts. Popcorn
1/2 cup Butter (melted)
1 pkg. Onion Soup Mix
2 tsp. Red Pepper Flakes

## Directions

Set warm popcorn aside. Pour butter over popcorn; dust with onion soup mix and pepper flakes; toss.

## Choco-Hot-Hot-Hot

### Ingredients

2 qts. Popcorn
3/4 cup Nestlés Chocolate Flavored Milk Mix
1/4 tsp. Cayenne Pepper
1 tsp. Cinnamon (ground)

### Directions

Set warm popcorn aside. Combine all other ingredients and mix.
Sprinkle over popcorn and toss to coat the kernels.

*Store popcorn kernels in an airtight container to avoid loss of moisture. Store in a cool dry place.*

## Wiki-Up Popcorn

### Ingredients

2 qts. Popcorn
1/3 cup Hot Sesame Seed Oil
1/4 cup Red Pepper Flakes

### Directions

Set warm popcorn aside. Heat hot sesame seed oil and drizzle over
popcorn. Toss kernels together. Sprinkle popcorn with red pepper
flakes.

# Explosive Popcorn

## Ingredients

2 qts. Popcorn
1/3 cup Butter (melted)
1/4 cup Hot Pepper Sauce
1 tsp. Soy Sauce
2 cups Spicy Snack Mix
1/2 package Bacon-Onion Mix

## Directions

Mix spicy snack mix with warm popcorn and set aside. Mix hot pepper sauce, soy sauce and melted butter. Pour butter mixture over popcorn and toss gently until kernels are evenly coated. Place on an oven tray in a 350° oven for 10 minutes. Stir as needed.

# Ah-h-h-h Popcorn

## Ingredients

2 qts. Popcorn
1/4 cup Hot Sesame Seed Oil
1/4 cup Butter (melted)
1 tsp. Garlic Powder

## Directions

Set warm popcorn aside. Mix hot sesame seed oil, butter, and garlic powder; drizzle over popcorn. Toss.

## Mouth-Puckering Popcorn

### Ingredients

2 1/2 qts. Popcorn
1/4 cup Butter (melted)
1/4 tsp. Cayenne Pepper
1/2 tsp. Garlic Powder
1 tsp. Lemon Pepper
1/2 tsp. Onion Powder
1 tsp. Paprika

### Directions

Pour melted butter over warm popcorn and set aside. Mix dry
ingredients together, then sprinkle over popcorn. Toss gently to
cover each kernel. Place on baking dish in 300° oven until crispy.
Stir as needed.

## Pitiquito Popcorn

### Ingredients

2 qts. Popcorn (air-popped)
Butter Flavored Cooking Spray
2 tsp. Chili Powder
2 tsp. Cumin
2 tsp. Paprika

### Directions

Place warm popcorn in a bowl. Spray popcorn using butter flavored cooking spray. Combine spices and sprinkle over popcorn.
Gently toss.

*Corn was extremely important to the Native American diet. The
Native Americans personified corn in their folklore and legends. They
referred to corn with names such as Corn Mother, Corn Maidens,
and Corn Grandfathers.*

# Yummy Popcorn Balls

## Ingredients

4 qts. Popcorn
1 cup Light Corn Syrup
1 small box Gelatin (any flavor)
1 cup Sugar

## Directions

Combine corn syrup, sugar and gelatin in a saucepan; bring to a
boil. Pour over popcorn and toss to coat evenly. Form into popcorn balls.

# Caramel Popcorn Balls

## Ingredients

2 qts. Popcorn
3 cups Rice Cereal (crispy)
1 bag Caramel Candy (unwrapped)
3 tbsp. Water
1 cup Peanuts (salted, shelled)
1/8 tsp. Salt

## Directions

Place popcorn and rice cereal in bowl; set aside. Combine caramel
candy and water in saucepan. Heat over low flame until melted. Or,
place caramel candy and water in microwave dish and heat until
melted. Add peanuts and salt. Pour caramel candy and peanut mixture over popcorn and cereal mixture; toss. Quickly form into popcorn balls.

## Fluffy Cloud Popcorn Balls

### Ingredients

6 qts. Popcorn
50 large Marshmallows (large bag)
1/3 cup Butter

### Directions

Place popcorn in a dish and set aside. Place marshmallows and butter in a saucepan. Heat over low flame until all is melted; stir as needed. Pour melted marshmallow / butter mixture over popcorn and toss. Form popcorn balls.


## Tom Turkey's Corn Balls

### Ingredients

5 qts. Popcorn (unsalted)
2 cups Sugar
1 cup Cranberry-Orange Relish (frozen)
1/2 cup Cranberry Juice
1/2 cup Light Corn Syrup
1 tsp. Vinegar
1/2 tsp. Salt

### Directions

Place popcorn in dish; set aside. Combine all remaining ingredients in a saucepan and bring to a boil. Cook to 250° on candy thermometer being careful not to let it boil over. Pour mixture over popcorn; toss. Let sit for 5 minutes to cool. Butter hands; form popcorn balls.

# Silly Tillie's Popcorn

## Ingredients

2 qts. Popcorn
1/3 cup Butter (melted)
1/2 cup Dried Tomatoes in Oil (chopped)
1 tbsp. Dried Basil

## Directions

Toss all ingredients together gently.

# Down East Balls

## Ingredients

4 qts. Popcorn
2 cups Sugar
2/3 cup Apple Juice
2/3 cup Maple Syrup
1/2 cup Butter
1 1/2 tsp. Salt
1 cup Peanuts (shelled)
1 1/2 cups Dates (chopped)
1 tsp. Vanilla Extract

## Directions

Place popcorn, peanuts and dates in a bowl; mix and set aside. In a saucepan bring to a boil: sugar, apple juice, syrup, butter and salt. Remove sugar from sides of pan with a wet brush. Continue cooking until mixture reaches 270° (Soft Crack Stage) on the candy thermometer. Add vanilla extract. Pour over popcorn mixture; toss well. Form popcorn balls.

## Basic Balls

### Ingredients

3 qts. Warm Popcorn
2 cups Sugar
1 1/2 cups Water
1/2 cup Light Corn Syrup
1 tsp. Vinegar
1/2 tsp. Salt
1 tsp. Vanilla Extract

### Directions

Place popcorn in a dish; place in 300° oven to keep warm. Place sugar, water, corn syrup, vinegar and salt in a large saucepan. Bring to 250° on candy thermometer (Hard Ball Stage). Add vanilla extract. Pour over popcorn and stir to coat well. Butter hands and form balls.

*The American Diabetes Association and the American Dietetic Association permit popcorn as a bread exchange on weight-control diets.*

## The Big Cheese Ball

### Ingredients

2 qts. Popcorn
2 tbsp. Butter
1/2 cup Cheddar Cheese (shredded)

### Directions

Place popcorn in bowl; set aside. Place butter and cheese in saucepan; melt. Drizzle over popcorn; toss. Form cheesy popcorn balls.

# Nutty Popcorn Balls

## Ingredients

4 qts. Popcorn
2 cups Nuts (peanuts, cashews, pecans)
3 cups Miniature Marshmallows
1 1/2 cups Gum Drops
1 cup Butter
1 1/3 cups Sugar
1/2 cup Light Corn Syrup
1 tsp. Vanilla Extract

## Directions

Combine popcorn, nuts, marshmallows and gum drops in a large bowl. Place butter in a saucepan and melt. Add sugar, corn syrup; bring to a boil and simmer for 3 minutes. Add vanilla extract. Stir. Pour over popcorn, toss and let cool for 2 minutes. Form popcorn balls.

# Bittersweet Balls

## Ingredients

5 qts. Popcorn
1 1/2 cups Sugar
1 1/4 cups Water
1 cup Orange Marmalade
1/2 tsp. Salt
1/2 cup Light Corn Syrup
1 tsp. Vinegar

## Directions

Place popcorn in a bowl; set aside. Bring sugar, water, marmalade, salt, corn syrup and vinegar to a boil in a saucepan; boil until sugar is dissolved. Bring mixture to 250° (Hard Ball Stage).  Pour over popcorn; toss. Form popcorn balls.

## Pucker-Up Popcorn

### Ingredients

2 qts. Popcorn (popped in oil)
2 tbsp. Lemon Zest
1 tsp. Dill Weed

### Directions

Combine all ingredients and toss.

## Tangy Popcorn

### Ingredients

2 1/2 qts. Popcorn
1 cup Yogurt (plain flavor)
1 cup Brown Sugar
1/3 cup Light Corn Syrup

### Directions

Place popcorn in a bowl and keep warm; set aside. Place yogurt, brown sugar and corn syrup in a saucepan. Bring to 250° (Hard Ball Stage) on candy thermometer. Pour over popcorn; toss to coat.

## Little Italy Popcorn

### Ingredients

2 1/2 qts. Popcorn (popped in oil)
1/2 pkg. Italian Salad Dressing Mix

### Directions

Place popcorn in a bowl and sprinkle with salad dressing mix. Toss until salad dressing mix coats popcorn very well.

# Beef-Jerky Popcorn

## Ingredients

3 qts. Popcorn (unsalted)
1 jar (2 1/2 oz.) Dried Beef (chopped)
1/2 cup Butter

## Directions

Combine dried beef and butter; cook for a few minutes. Pour mixture over popcorn and toss. Serve while hot.

*The American Dental Association lists popcorn as a sugar-free snack.*

# Peanut Butter Popcorn

## Ingredients

4 qts. Popcorn (salted)
1/2 cup Sugar
3/4 cup Light Corn Syrup
3/4 cup Peanut Butter
1 tsp. Vanilla Extract

## Directions

Place sugar and corn syrup in saucepan; boil until sugar is dissolved. Remove from heat. Add peanut butter and vanilla extract. Pour over popcorn; mix well.

## Nutty-Chocolate Popcorn Treat

### Ingredients

8 qts. Popcorn
3 cups Sugar
1/2 cup Light Corn Syrup
1/2 cup Dark Corn Syrup
2/3 cup Water
6 tbsp. Butter
1/2 tsp. Vanilla Extract
1 pkg. Semi-sweet Chocolate Chips
1 cup Almonds (toasted and slivered)

### Directions

Place popcorn in two roasting pans. Combine sugar, corn syrups and water in a saucepan; bring to boil. Add butter and stir as needed until temperature reaches 300°–310° on candy thermometer. When it can form hard brittle threads, the mixture is ready. Remove from heat and add salt, baking soda and vanilla extract. Beware of splattering and foaming at this stage. Pour over popcorn and cool. Break into large chunks. Melt semi-sweet chocolate chips, pour over popcorn and sprinkle with slivered almonds. Let chocolate harden.

*A 1912 party book featured instructions for a "Popcorn Frolic". Party goers ate popcorn and played popcorn games called "corn-drop", "popcorn races", and "popcorn hunt".*

# Red Popcorn

## Ingredients

3 qts. Popcorn
2 cups White Sugar
2 tbsp. Butter
6 tbsp. Water
Red Food Coloring

## Directions

Combine sugar, butter, water, and red food coloring. Bring to Soft Boil. Drizzle over popcorn; stir.

# Hot Cinnamon Balls

## Ingredients

8 qts. Popcorn
2 lbs. Sugar
1 cup Light Corn Syrup
1/4 lb. Margarine
2 tsp. Cinnamon Oil
1 tsp. Red Food Coloring
1 cup Red-Hot Candies

## Directions

Bring sugar, syrup and margarine to Hard Crack Stage. Add cinnamon oil and red food coloring. Pour over popcorn; toss. Slightly cool and add red-hot candies. Form balls.

*Native Americans use corn husks, pollen, kernels and entire corn ears in tribal ceremonies celebrating corn planting and harvesting.*

## On-A-Shoestring Popcorn

### Ingredients

1/3 cup Popping Corn (popped)
1 cup Mixed Nuts (shelled)
2 cups Shoestring Potatoes
1/3 cup Butter (melted)
1 tsp. Dill Weed
1 tsp. Lemon Pepper
1 tsp. Worcestershire Sauce
1/2 tsp. Garlic Powder
1/2 tsp. Onion Powder
1/4 tsp. Salt

### Directions

Mix popcorn, nuts and shoestring potatoes; set aside. Mix butter and seasoning; drizzle over popcorn mixture; toss. Place on baking sheet and bake in 350° oven for 5-7 minutes. Stir one time.

## Corn Cubed

### Ingredients

3 qts. Popcorn
3 cups Corn Chex Cereal Mix
3 cups Corn Chips (broken)
1 pkg. (11 oz.) Butterscotch Chips
3/4 lb. Dark Chocolate Candy Coating

### Directions

Combine the three corns: popcorn, Chex Cereal Mix and corn chips. Set aside. Melt butterscotch chips and chocolate candy coating in a saucepan over low heat. Pour over popcorn mixture and toss. Put into (2) greased 15" by 10" baking pans. Cut or break when cool.

## Bouquet Garni Popcorn

### Ingredients

1 pkg. Microwave Popcorn
2 tbsp. Butter
1/2 tsp. Basil
1/4 tsp. Oregano
1/4 tsp. Onion Powder
1/8 tsp. Garlic Powder
2 tbsp. Parmesan Cheese

### Directions

Prepare microwave popcorn as directed. Place in bowl. Combine basil, oregano, onion and garlic powders with butter and microwave until butter is melted. Pour over popcorn and then sprinkle with cheese. Toss.

## Super Red Popcorn

### Ingredients

2 1/2 qts. Popcorn (air-popped)
Buttery Flavored Cooking Spray
1 pkg. Flavored Gelatin (red)

### Directions

Place hot popcorn in a bowl and lightly spray with cooking spray. Sprinkle red gelatin mix on popcorn and toss. Place in 350° oven for 5 minutes.

*When you purchase microwave popcorn be sure to check the salt and fat content on the package.*

*Use a little butter to "grease" your hands when you want to form pop-corn balls. This will prevent the hot popcorn from sticking to your hands, and you will be able to work quickly.*

## Crumb Crunchers' Popcorn

### Ingredients

4 qts. Popcorn
Salt (Butter Flavored)
Nuts (Peanuts, Almonds, Walnuts, Pecans)
Dried Fruit (Raisins, Apricots, Dates)
Pumpkin Seeds
Chocolate Chip Morsels or Carob Morsels

### Directions

Place salted popcorn in a bowl. Select any of the other ingredients to add to the popcorn and toss.

## Health Food Nuts

### Ingredients

2 1/2 qts. Popcorn
2 tbsp. Sunflower Kernels (ground)
2 tbsp. Almonds (ground)
2 tbsp. Walnuts (ground)
2 tbsp. Wheat Germ
6 tbsp. Butter (melted)
1 2/3 cups Dried Fruit (diced)

### Directions

Place popcorn in a bowl; set aside. Drizzle butter over popcorn; toss. Mix in dried fruit, ground nuts and wheat germ.

## Pat-A-Cake Popcorn

### Ingredients

2 1/2 qts. Popcorn (air-popped)
1 cup Non-Fat Yogurt (plain flavor)
3/4 cup Pancake Syrup (light)
2 tsp. Maple Extract

### Directions

Place popcorn in a bowl, keep warm and set aside. In a saucepan, combine yogurt and pancake syrup. Bring to 225° on candy thermometer; remove immediately. Add maple extract and drizzle over popcorn. Stir to coat.

## Sweet William's Corn

### Ingredients

1/2 cup of Popcorn kernels
1/4 cup Corn Oil
3 tbsp. Granulated Sugar

### Directions

Place the oil in a pan and heat. Add popcorn kernels to hot oil. Sprinkle the granulated sugar over popcorn kernels in the pan before the kernels pop. Cover and pop the corn kernels, remembering to continue shaking the pan over the heat until all the kernels are popped.

*A popular 19th century method of cooking popcorn was to put popcorn kernels in a kettle full of lard. When the corn popped, it was skimmed off the surface of the lard and eaten.*

## Gooey Messy Popcorn

### Ingredients

3 qts. Popcorn
1/2 cup Butter
1/2 cup Brown Sugar

### Directions

Place the popcorn in a baking dish; set aside. Combine the butter and brown sugar. Whip together until nice and creamy. Add this mixture to the popcorn. Toss until popcorn is lightly coated with sugar and butter mixture. Place in oven of 350° for five or more minutes until popcorn is crispy. Delicious!

## Zesty Cheese Popcorn

### Ingredients

2 qts. Popcorn
3 tbsp. Butter
1/2 tsp. Chili Powder
1/2 tsp. Garlic Salt
1/4 tsp. Onion Powder
1/2 cup Parmesan Cheese (grated)

### Directions

Combine melted butter, chili powder, garlic salt, and the onion powder. Pour mixture over the popped corn and sprinkle with Parmesan cheese. Toss gently.

# Zenobia's Popcorn Balls

## Ingredients

2 qts. Popcorn (plain)
1 cup Light Corn Syrup
1 cup Granulated Sugar
1/4 cup Cold Water
2 tsp. Vinegar
1/4 tsp. Salt
1 tbsp. Butter

## Directions

Combine corn syrup, granulated sugar, water, vinegar and salt in a sauce pan. Stir over medium heat until boiling and it reaches 260°. Pour this mixture over the popcorn and toss until corn is lightly coated. Allow popcorn to cool. Form popcorn into balls or place in a greased cake pan to cut into bars when completely cool.

# Mejicano Popcorn

## Ingredients

2 qts. Popcorn
3 tbsp. Butter (melted)
1 tbsp. Dried Taco Seasoning Mix
1/2 tsp. Dried, Chopped Chives
Salt to taste

## Directions

Set popcorn aside. Pour over popcorn and toss.

## Chicken Feed Popcorn

### Ingredients

2 qts. Popcorn
3 tbsp. Butter (melted)
2 pkgs. Broth Mix (chicken flavored)
1 tsp. Instant Minced Onion
1 tsp. Parsley Flakes
1/2 tsp. Sage (ground)

### Directions

Set popcorn aside. Combine all other ingredients together and pour over popcorn. Gently toss.

## Baco-Cheezo Popcorn

### Ingredients

2 1/2 qts. Popcorn
6 slices Bacon (fried crispy and crumbled)
4 oz. Cheddar Cheese (grated)

### Directions

Combine all ingredients in a large bowl and toss.

## Count Dracula Popcorn

### Ingredients

2 qts. Popcorn
1/4 cup Butter (melted)
1 tbsp. Garlic Salt

Directions
Place the popped popcorn in a large, flat pan.
Pour melted butter over popcorn
Sprinkle liberally with garlic salt.
Warm in 350° oven for 10-15 minutes. Eat hot.

## Pop-A-Roons

### Ingredients

1 cup Popcorn
1 cup Nuts (your choice; finely chopped)
3 Egg Whites
1 cup Powdered Sugar
3/4 tsp. Vanilla Extract

### Directions

Finely chop the popcorn in a blender. Place popcorn and nuts in a bowl. Beat the egg white until foamy, add sugar and beat until stiff peaks are formed. Gently fold in popcorn and nuts mixture, then stir in vanilla extract. Drop by spoonfuls onto a lightly oiled cookie sheet. Preheat oven to 300° then bake for 30-35 minutes.

## Gotta-Have-Chocolate Popcorn

### Ingredients

2 qts. Popcorn
1 cup Granulated Sugar
1/2 cup Water
1/3 cup Corn Syrup
1/4 tsp. Salt
3 tbsp. Margarine
1/3 cup Chocolate pieces
1 tsp. Vanilla Extract

### Directions

Place popcorn in a lightly greased bowl. Mix sugar, water, corn syrup and salt together and cook over moderate heat until mixtures reaches 240° on a candy thermometer. Add vanilla extract and chocolate pieces. Drizzle hot chocolate mixture over popcorn. Toss until corn is coated and syrup loses the glossy look. Cool and store in container. Do not refrigerate.

## About the Author

Victor E. Cheer was born and reared in rural Upstate New York. At a very young age his extended family relocated and he suddenly found himself a resident of the busy Upper West Side of Manhattan. There he was to explore a whole new world through the eyes of a child.

From early on, he was interested in nature, science and tinkering. His early childhood days had been filled with camping trips, weenie roasts, marshmallows toasted on twigs, hobo-popcorn, and an elaborate plan to create a machine that would explode the popcorn using recycled steam. Now he explored the trails of Central Park, learned the names of birds, and looked for worms in water puddles along the sidewalks. When winter came and it was time to hibernate, he turned to the kitchen to explore his culinary talents. There, amid puffs of white flour clouds, he created the tastiest, lightest blueberry pancakes known to his family and friends.

It wasn't long before he had taken up exploring the art of popcorn popping. If there had been an award for testing all the popcorn varieties available he certainly would have received it. The challenge of finding the correct oil temperature, the best popping pan, and the best variety of popcorn was one he couldn't resist. If he didn't eat the popcorn while watching a home video, he would creatively study each popped kernel to discover a wild animal shape or trigger an idea for a new invention.

Inevitably Victor was dubbed "Mr. Pencil". He always had to carry one sharpened pencil, just in case, tucked behind his ear. He'd always kept his notebook filled with special words, lists, new recipes, drawings of inventions, and various unrelated topics to explore.

He recently confided that his next literary project would be a compilation of tasty campfire recipes. But before that book is published, he will personally supervise every taste test.

## Find Special Popcorn

Black Shield, Inc.
5356 Pan Amer. Fwy NE
Albuquerque, NM 87109
(800) 653-9357

Cathy's Country Store
2125 N. Richmond St.
Appleton, WI 54911
(920) 830-3311

Chester's Popcorn Store
401 East US Hwy 30
Valparaiso, IN 46383
(219) 462-1131

Fisher's Popcorn
200 South Boardwalk
Ocean City, MD 21842
(410) 289-5638

Garrett Popcorn Shops
Box 11342
Chicago, IL 60611
(888) 476-7267

Gisi's Gourmet Popcorn
46240 South Shore Drive
Wentworth, SD 57075
(605) 489-2535

Karmelkorn
320 Northtown Drive
Blaine, MN 55434
(612) 780-2807

Myers Gourmet Popcorn
8025 W. Hwy 24
Cascade, CO 80809
(800) 684-1155

Noble Popcorn Farms
P.O. Box 157
401 N. 13th Street
Sac City, IA 50583
(800) 537-9554

Popcorn Factory
P.O. Box 4530
Lake Bluff, IL 60044
(800) 541-2676

Popcorn World, Inc.
P.O. Box 507
2303 Princeton Road
Trenton, MO 64683
(800) 443-8226

Pop 'N Stuff Inc.
1303 Celebrity Circle E-125
Myrtle Beach, SC 29577
(843) 444-4680

Rural Route 1 Popcorn
RR 1 Hwy. 80
Livingston, WI 53554
(800) 828-8115

South Dakota Popcorn Company
2750 Industrial Road #3
Pierre, SD 57501
(800) 535-2909

Vic's Corn Popper
14418 West Center Road
Omaha, NE 68144
(877) 330-8427

## Pippity-Poppity Popcorn Book
## Collectible Commemorative Encased Cent

First in an advertising series from the Presbyopian Press!
These beautiful good luck charms are circular, anodized a shiny
watery blue, and encase an Indian head penny or buffalo nickel.
They joyfully celebrate Native American Culture.
The obverse side features: Book Title, ISBN, Author's name, art-
work depicting two boxes of popcorn. The reverse side features:
Press Name, City/State/Website Address, artwork depicting the
Press Logo of telescopes.
These pieces are signed by designer Bryan G. Ryker, have a mintage
of 500 each, and were produced by Gage Corporation.

Yes! I'm ordering:
_____encased Indian head cents      _____encased buffalo nickels

at $5.00 each and FREE SHIPPING!

Please charge my:

Visa _____Exp_____

MasterCard _____Exp_____

My check or money order for $_____is enclosed.

Name_____
Organization_____
Address_____
City/State/Zip_____
Phone_____Email_____

Card #_____Exp. Date____

Please make your check payable and return to:
Presbyopian Press
P.O. Box 563
Hackensack, NJ 07602-0563

## A New Gift for Popcorn Lovers—
## The Pippity-Poppity Popcorn Book

Available at leading bookstores, or order here.

Yes! I'm ordering:

_____ copies of The Pippity-Poppity Popcorn Book

   at $2.95 each, plus $1.50 shipping.

Please charge my:

Visa _____Exp_____

MasterCard _____Exp_____

My check or money order for $_____is enclosed.

Name_____
Organization_____
Address_____
City/State/Zip_____
Phone_____Email_____

Card #_____Exp. Date_____

Please make your check payable and return to:
Presbyopian Press
P.O. Box 563
Hackensack, NJ 07602-0563